ADDRESS BOOK
CHRISTIAN

The Pocket Size Address Book

All rights reserved. No part of this document may be reproduced or transmitted in any form or by any means, electronic or otherwise. This means that you cannot record or photocopy any material Ideas, tips or suggestions that are provided in this book

www.journalsrus.com

Address Book Christian
© 2016 Ciparum LLC
All rights reserved.
ISBN-10:1-63589-045-4
ISBN-13:978-1-63589-045-7

Table of Content

Name	Page	Name	Page
John Doe	*24*		

Name	Page	Name	Page

Name	Page	Name	Page

THIS PAGE WAS
INTENTIONALLY
LEFT BLANK

NAME..
ADDRESS...
....
MOBILE # (Cell)...
HOME #..
WORK #..
FAX...
EMAIL..

NAME..
ADDRESS...
....
MOBILE # (Cell)...
HOME #..
WORK #..
FAX...
EMAIL..

NAME..
ADDRESS...
....
MOBILE # (Cell)...
HOME #..
WORK #..
FAX...
EMAIL..

NOTES:

NAME..
ADDRESS...
....
MOBILE # (Cell)..
HOME #..
WORK #..
FAX...
EMAIL..

NAME..
ADDRESS...
....
MOBILE # (Cell)..
HOME #..
WORK #..
FAX...
EMAIL..

NAME..
ADDRESS...
....
MOBILE # (Cell)..
HOME #..
WORK #..
FAX...
EMAIL..

NOTES:

NAME..
ADDRESS..
....
MOBILE # (Cell)..
HOME #..
WORK #..
FAX..
EMAIL..

NAME..
ADDRESS..
....
MOBILE # (Cell)..
HOME #..
WORK #..
FAX..
EMAIL..

NAME..
ADDRESS..
....
MOBILE # (Cell)..
HOME #..
WORK #..
FAX..
EMAIL..

NOTES:

NAME..
ADDRESS..
....
MOBILE # (Cell)...
HOME #..
WORK #..
FAX...
EMAIL..

NAME..
ADDRESS..
....
MOBILE # (Cell)...
HOME #..
WORK #..
FAX...
EMAIL..

NAME..
ADDRESS..
....
MOBILE # (Cell)...
HOME #..
WORK #..
FAX...
EMAIL..

NOTES:

NAME..
ADDRESS...
....
MOBILE # (Cell)...
HOME #..
WORK #..
FAX...
EMAIL..

NAME..
ADDRESS...
....
MOBILE # (Cell)...
HOME #..
WORK #..
FAX...
EMAIL..

NAME..
ADDRESS...
....
MOBILE # (Cell)...
HOME #..
WORK #..
FAX...
EMAIL..

NOTES:

NAME..
ADDRESS..
....
MOBILE # (Cell)...
HOME #...
WORK #...
FAX..
EMAIL..

NAME..
ADDRESS..
....
MOBILE # (Cell)...
HOME #...
WORK #...
FAX..
EMAIL..

NAME..
ADDRESS..
....
MOBILE # (Cell)...
HOME #...
WORK #...
FAX..
EMAIL..

NOTES:

NAME..
ADDRESS..
....
MOBILE # (Cell)...
HOME #..
WORK #..
FAX...
EMAIL...

NAME..
ADDRESS..
....
MOBILE # (Cell)...
HOME #..
WORK #..
FAX...
EMAIL...

NAME..
ADDRESS..
....
MOBILE # (Cell)...
HOME #..
WORK #..
FAX...
EMAIL...

NOTES:

NAME..
ADDRESS..
....
MOBILE # (Cell)...
HOME #..
WORK #..
FAX...
EMAIL..

NAME..
ADDRESS..
....
MOBILE # (Cell)...
HOME #..
WORK #..
FAX...
EMAIL..

NAME..
ADDRESS..
....
MOBILE # (Cell)...
HOME #..
WORK #..
FAX...
EMAIL..

NOTES:

NAME..
ADDRESS..
....
MOBILE # (Cell)...
HOME #..
WORK #..
FAX..
EMAIL...

NAME..
ADDRESS..
....
MOBILE # (Cell)...
HOME #..
WORK #..
FAX..
EMAIL...

NAME..
ADDRESS..
....
MOBILE # (Cell)...
HOME #..
WORK #..
FAX..
EMAIL...

NOTES:

NAME..
ADDRESS...
....
MOBILE # (Cell)..
HOME #...
WORK #..
FAX...
EMAIL..

NAME..
ADDRESS...
....
MOBILE # (Cell)..
HOME #...
WORK #..
FAX...
EMAIL..

NAME..
ADDRESS...
....
MOBILE # (Cell)..
HOME #...
WORK #..
FAX...
EMAIL..

NOTES:

NAME..
ADDRESS..
....
MOBILE # (Cell)...
HOME #..
WORK #...
FAX...
EMAIL..

NAME..
ADDRESS..
....
MOBILE # (Cell)...
HOME #..
WORK #...
FAX...
EMAIL..

NAME..
ADDRESS..
....
MOBILE # (Cell)...
HOME #..
WORK #...
FAX...
EMAIL..

NOTES:

NAME..
ADDRESS..
....
MOBILE # (Cell)..
HOME #..
WORK #..
FAX...
EMAIL...

NAME..
ADDRESS..
....
MOBILE # (Cell)..
HOME #..
WORK #..
FAX...
EMAIL...

NAME..
ADDRESS..
....
MOBILE # (Cell)..
HOME #..
WORK #..
FAX...
EMAIL...

NOTES:

NAME..
ADDRESS..
....
MOBILE # (Cell)..
HOME #...
WORK #...
FAX..
EMAIL...

NAME..
ADDRESS..
....
MOBILE # (Cell)..
HOME #...
WORK #...
FAX..
EMAIL...

NAME..
ADDRESS..
....
MOBILE # (Cell)..
HOME #...
WORK #...
FAX..
EMAIL...

NOTES:

NAME..
ADDRESS..
....
MOBILE # (Cell)...
HOME #..
WORK #..
FAX..
EMAIL...

NAME..
ADDRESS..
....
MOBILE # (Cell)...
HOME #..
WORK #..
FAX..
EMAIL...

NAME..
ADDRESS..
....
MOBILE # (Cell)...
HOME #..
WORK #..
FAX..
EMAIL...

NOTES:

NAME..
ADDRESS..
....
MOBILE # (Cell)...
HOME #...
WORK #...
FAX..
EMAIL...

NAME..
ADDRESS..
....
MOBILE # (Cell)...
HOME #...
WORK #...
FAX..
EMAIL...

NAME..
ADDRESS..
....
MOBILE # (Cell)...
HOME #...
WORK #...
FAX..
EMAIL...

NOTES:

NAME..
ADDRESS..
....
MOBILE # (Cell)...
HOME #..
WORK #..
FAX..
EMAIL..

NAME..
ADDRESS..
....
MOBILE # (Cell)...
HOME #..
WORK #..
FAX..
EMAIL..

NAME..
ADDRESS..
....
MOBILE # (Cell)...
HOME #..
WORK #..
FAX..
EMAIL..

NOTES:

NAME..
ADDRESS..
....
MOBILE # (Cell)...
HOME #..
WORK #..
FAX...
EMAIL..

NAME..
ADDRESS..
....
MOBILE # (Cell)...
HOME #..
WORK #..
FAX...
EMAIL..

NAME..
ADDRESS..
....
MOBILE # (Cell)...
HOME #..
WORK #..
FAX...
EMAIL..

NOTES:

NAME..
ADDRESS...
....
MOBILE # (Cell)...
HOME #..
WORK #..
FAX...
EMAIL...

NAME..
ADDRESS...
....
MOBILE # (Cell)...
HOME #..
WORK #..
FAX...
EMAIL...

NAME..
ADDRESS...
....
MOBILE # (Cell)...
HOME #..
WORK #..
FAX...
EMAIL...

NOTES:

NAME..
ADDRESS...
....
MOBILE # (Cell)...
HOME #...
WORK #...
FAX...
EMAIL..

NAME..
ADDRESS...
....
MOBILE # (Cell)...
HOME #...
WORK #...
FAX...
EMAIL..

NAME..
ADDRESS...
....
MOBILE # (Cell)...
HOME #...
WORK #...
FAX...
EMAIL..

NOTES:

NAME..
ADDRESS..
....
MOBILE # (Cell)..
HOME #..
WORK #...
FAX...
EMAIL..

NAME..
ADDRESS..
....
MOBILE # (Cell)..
HOME #..
WORK #...
FAX...
EMAIL..

NAME..
ADDRESS..
....
MOBILE # (Cell)..
HOME #..
WORK #...
FAX...
EMAIL..

NOTES:

NAME...
ADDRESS...
....
MOBILE # (Cell)...
HOME #..
WORK #..
FAX..
EMAIL..

NAME...
ADDRESS...
....
MOBILE # (Cell)...
HOME #..
WORK #..
FAX..
EMAIL..

NAME...
ADDRESS...
....
MOBILE # (Cell)...
HOME #..
WORK #..
FAX..
EMAIL..

NOTES:

NAME..
ADDRESS..
....
MOBILE # (Cell)..
HOME #..
WORK #..
FAX...
EMAIL...

NAME..
ADDRESS..
....
MOBILE # (Cell)..
HOME #..
WORK #..
FAX...
EMAIL...

NAME..
ADDRESS..
....
MOBILE # (Cell)..
HOME #..
WORK #..
FAX...
EMAIL...

NOTES:

NAME..
ADDRESS...
....
MOBILE # (Cell)...
HOME #..
WORK #..
FAX..
EMAIL...

NAME..
ADDRESS...
....
MOBILE # (Cell)...
HOME #..
WORK #..
FAX..
EMAIL...

NAME..
ADDRESS...
....
MOBILE # (Cell)...
HOME #..
WORK #..
FAX..
EMAIL...

NOTES:

NAME..
ADDRESS...
....
MOBILE # (Cell)..
HOME #..
WORK #..
FAX..
EMAIL..

NAME..
ADDRESS...
....
MOBILE # (Cell)..
HOME #..
WORK #..
FAX..
EMAIL..

NAME..
ADDRESS...
....
MOBILE # (Cell)..
HOME #..
WORK #..
FAX..
EMAIL..

NOTES:

NAME..
ADDRESS..
....
MOBILE # (Cell)..
HOME #...
WORK #..
FAX...
EMAIL...

NAME..
ADDRESS..
....
MOBILE # (Cell)..
HOME #...
WORK #..
FAX...
EMAIL...

NAME..
ADDRESS..
....
MOBILE # (Cell)..
HOME #...
WORK #..
FAX...
EMAIL...

NOTES:

NAME..
ADDRESS..
....
MOBILE # (Cell)..
HOME #...
WORK #...
FAX...
EMAIL..

NAME..
ADDRESS..
....
MOBILE # (Cell)..
HOME #...
WORK #...
FAX...
EMAIL..

NAME..
ADDRESS..
....
MOBILE # (Cell)..
HOME #...
WORK #...
FAX...
EMAIL..

NOTES:

NAME………………………………………………………………
ADDRESS……………………………………………………………...
………………………………………………………………………....
MOBILE # (Cell)……………………………………………………..…..
HOME #………………………………………………………………..…...
WORK #……………………………………………………………..........
FAX…………………………………………………………………………..
EMAIL………………………………………………………………………..

NAME………………………………………………………………
ADDRESS……………………………………………………………...
………………………………………………………………………....
MOBILE # (Cell)……………………………………………………..…..
HOME #………………………………………………………………..…...
WORK #……………………………………………………………..........
FAX…………………………………………………………………………..
EMAIL………………………………………………………………………..

NAME………………………………………………………………
ADDRESS……………………………………………………………...
………………………………………………………………………....
MOBILE # (Cell)……………………………………………………..…..
HOME #………………………………………………………………..…...
WORK #……………………………………………………………..........
FAX…………………………………………………………………………..
EMAIL………………………………………………………………………..

NOTES:

NAME..
ADDRESS...
....
MOBILE # (Cell)..
HOME #..
WORK #..
FAX...
EMAIL..

NAME..
ADDRESS...
....
MOBILE # (Cell)..
HOME #..
WORK #..
FAX...
EMAIL..

NAME..
ADDRESS...
....
MOBILE # (Cell)..
HOME #..
WORK #..
FAX...
EMAIL..

NOTES:

NAME..
ADDRESS..
....
MOBILE # (Cell)..
HOME #...
WORK #...
FAX..
EMAIL...

NAME..
ADDRESS..
....
MOBILE # (Cell)..
HOME #...
WORK #...
FAX..
EMAIL...

NAME..
ADDRESS..
....
MOBILE # (Cell)..
HOME #...
WORK #...
FAX..
EMAIL...

NOTES:

NAME..
ADDRESS..
....
MOBILE # (Cell)...
HOME #..
WORK #..
FAX...
EMAIL..

NAME..
ADDRESS..
....
MOBILE # (Cell)...
HOME #..
WORK #..
FAX...
EMAIL..

NAME..
ADDRESS..
....
MOBILE # (Cell)...
HOME #..
WORK #..
FAX...
EMAIL..

NOTES:

NAME..
ADDRESS..
....
MOBILE # (Cell)..
HOME #..
WORK #..
FAX...
EMAIL..

NAME..
ADDRESS..
....
MOBILE # (Cell)..
HOME #..
WORK #..
FAX...
EMAIL..

NAME..
ADDRESS..
....
MOBILE # (Cell)..
HOME #..
WORK #..
FAX...
EMAIL..

NOTES:

NAME..
ADDRESS..
....
MOBILE # (Cell)..
HOME #...
WORK #...
FAX..
EMAIL..

NAME..
ADDRESS..
....
MOBILE # (Cell)..
HOME #...
WORK #...
FAX..
EMAIL..

NAME..
ADDRESS..
....
MOBILE # (Cell)..
HOME #...
WORK #...
FAX..
EMAIL..

NOTES:

NAME..
ADDRESS..
....
MOBILE # (Cell)..
HOME #..
WORK #..
FAX...
EMAIL...

NAME..
ADDRESS..
....
MOBILE # (Cell)..
HOME #..
WORK #..
FAX...
EMAIL...

NAME..
ADDRESS..
....
MOBILE # (Cell)..
HOME #..
WORK #..
FAX...
EMAIL...

NOTES:

NAME..
ADDRESS...
....
MOBILE # (Cell)...
HOME #..
WORK #..
FAX..
EMAIL..

NAME..
ADDRESS...
....
MOBILE # (Cell)...
HOME #..
WORK #..
FAX..
EMAIL..

NAME..
ADDRESS...
....
MOBILE # (Cell)...
HOME #..
WORK #..
FAX..
EMAIL..

NOTES:

NAME..
ADDRESS..
....
MOBILE # (Cell)...
HOME #..
WORK #..
FAX...
EMAIL..

NAME..
ADDRESS..
....
MOBILE # (Cell)...
HOME #..
WORK #..
FAX...
EMAIL..

NAME..
ADDRESS..
....
MOBILE # (Cell)...
HOME #..
WORK #..
FAX...
EMAIL..

NOTES:

NAME..
ADDRESS...
....
MOBILE # (Cell)...
HOME #...
WORK #...
FAX..
EMAIL..

NAME..
ADDRESS...
....
MOBILE # (Cell)...
HOME #...
WORK #...
FAX..
EMAIL..

NAME..
ADDRESS...
....
MOBILE # (Cell)...
HOME #...
WORK #...
FAX..
EMAIL..

NOTES:

NAME..
ADDRESS..
....
MOBILE # (Cell)...
HOME #...
WORK #...
FAX..
EMAIL...

NAME..
ADDRESS..
....
MOBILE # (Cell)...
HOME #...
WORK #...
FAX..
EMAIL...

NAME..
ADDRESS..
....
MOBILE # (Cell)...
HOME #...
WORK #...
FAX..
EMAIL...

NOTES:

NAME..
ADDRESS..
....
MOBILE # (Cell)...
HOME #...
WORK #..
FAX..
EMAIL..

NAME..
ADDRESS..
....
MOBILE # (Cell)...
HOME #...
WORK #..
FAX..
EMAIL..

NAME..
ADDRESS..
....
MOBILE # (Cell)...
HOME #...
WORK #..
FAX..
EMAIL..

NOTES:

NAME..
ADDRESS..
....
MOBILE # (Cell)..
HOME #...
WORK #...
FAX..
EMAIL..

NAME..
ADDRESS..
....
MOBILE # (Cell)..
HOME #...
WORK #...
FAX..
EMAIL..

NAME..
ADDRESS..
....
MOBILE # (Cell)..
HOME #...
WORK #...
FAX..
EMAIL..

NOTES:

NAME..
ADDRESS...
....
MOBILE # (Cell)...
HOME #...
WORK #...
FAX..
EMAIL..

NAME..
ADDRESS...
....
MOBILE # (Cell)...
HOME #...
WORK #...
FAX..
EMAIL..

NAME..
ADDRESS...
....
MOBILE # (Cell)...
HOME #...
WORK #...
FAX..
EMAIL..

NOTES:

NAME..
ADDRESS..
....
MOBILE # (Cell)..
HOME #..
WORK #..
FAX..
EMAIL...

NAME..
ADDRESS..
....
MOBILE # (Cell)..
HOME #..
WORK #..
FAX..
EMAIL...

NAME..
ADDRESS..
....
MOBILE # (Cell)..
HOME #..
WORK #..
FAX..
EMAIL...

NOTES:

NAME..
ADDRESS..
....
MOBILE # (Cell)...
HOME #..
WORK #..
FAX...
EMAIL...

NAME..
ADDRESS..
....
MOBILE # (Cell)...
HOME #..
WORK #..
FAX...
EMAIL...

NAME..
ADDRESS..
....
MOBILE # (Cell)...
HOME #..
WORK #..
FAX...
EMAIL...

NOTES:

NAME..
ADDRESS...
....
MOBILE # (Cell)..…..
HOME #..…..…
WORK #...….........
FAX..…..
EMAIL..…..

NAME..
ADDRESS...
....
MOBILE # (Cell)..…..
HOME #..…..…
WORK #...….........
FAX..…..
EMAIL..…..

NAME..
ADDRESS...
....
MOBILE # (Cell)..…..
HOME #..…..…
WORK #...….........
FAX..…..
EMAIL..…..

NOTES:

NAME..
ADDRESS..
....
MOBILE # (Cell)..
HOME #..
WORK #..
FAX..
EMAIL..

NAME..
ADDRESS..
....
MOBILE # (Cell)..
HOME #..
WORK #..
FAX..
EMAIL..

NAME..
ADDRESS..
....
MOBILE # (Cell)..
HOME #..
WORK #..
FAX..
EMAIL..

NOTES:

NAME………………………………………………………………
ADDRESS……………………………………………………………...
………………………………………………………………………....
MOBILE # (Cell)……………………………………………………..
HOME #……………………………………………………………...
WORK #………………………………………………………….......
FAX…………………………………………………………………..
EMAIL………………………………………………………………..

NAME………………………………………………………………
ADDRESS……………………………………………………………...
………………………………………………………………………....
MOBILE # (Cell)……………………………………………………..
HOME #……………………………………………………………...
WORK #………………………………………………………….......
FAX…………………………………………………………………..
EMAIL………………………………………………………………..

NAME………………………………………………………………
ADDRESS……………………………………………………………...
………………………………………………………………………....
MOBILE # (Cell)……………………………………………………..
HOME #……………………………………………………………...
WORK #………………………………………………………….......
FAX…………………………………………………………………..
EMAIL………………………………………………………………..

NOTES:

NAME..
ADDRESS..
....
MOBILE # (Cell)...
HOME #..
WORK #..
FAX..
EMAIL...

NAME..
ADDRESS..
....
MOBILE # (Cell)...
HOME #..
WORK #..
FAX..
EMAIL...

NAME..
ADDRESS..
....
MOBILE # (Cell)...
HOME #..
WORK #..
FAX..
EMAIL...

NOTES:

NAME..
ADDRESS...
....
MOBILE # (Cell)..
HOME #...
WORK #...
FAX...
EMAIL..

NAME..
ADDRESS...
....
MOBILE # (Cell)..
HOME #...
WORK #...
FAX...
EMAIL..

NAME..
ADDRESS...
....
MOBILE # (Cell)..
HOME #...
WORK #...
FAX...
EMAIL..

NOTES:

NAME..
ADDRESS...
....
MOBILE # (Cell)..
HOME #..
WORK #..
FAX...
EMAIL..

NAME..
ADDRESS...
....
MOBILE # (Cell)..
HOME #..
WORK #..
FAX...
EMAIL..

NAME..
ADDRESS...
....
MOBILE # (Cell)..
HOME #..
WORK #..
FAX...
EMAIL..

NOTES:

NAME..
ADDRESS...
....
MOBILE # (Cell)...
HOME #..
WORK #..
FAX..
EMAIL..

NAME..
ADDRESS...
....
MOBILE # (Cell)...
HOME #..
WORK #..
FAX..
EMAIL..

NAME..
ADDRESS...
....
MOBILE # (Cell)...
HOME #..
WORK #..
FAX..
EMAIL..

NOTES:

NAME..
ADDRESS..
....
MOBILE # (Cell)..
HOME #..
WORK #..
FAX..
EMAIL..

NAME..
ADDRESS..
....
MOBILE # (Cell)..
HOME #..
WORK #..
FAX..
EMAIL..

NAME..
ADDRESS..
....
MOBILE # (Cell)..
HOME #..
WORK #..
FAX..
EMAIL..

NOTES:

NAME..
ADDRESS..
....
MOBILE # (Cell)...
HOME #...
WORK #...
FAX..
EMAIL..

NAME..
ADDRESS..
....
MOBILE # (Cell)...
HOME #...
WORK #...
FAX..
EMAIL..

NAME..
ADDRESS..
....
MOBILE # (Cell)...
HOME #...
WORK #...
FAX..
EMAIL..

NOTES:

NAME..
ADDRESS..
....
MOBILE # (Cell)...
HOME #...
WORK #...
FAX...
EMAIL..

NAME..
ADDRESS..
....
MOBILE # (Cell)...
HOME #...
WORK #...
FAX...
EMAIL..

NAME..
ADDRESS..
....
MOBILE # (Cell)...
HOME #...
WORK #...
FAX...
EMAIL..

NOTES:

NAME..
ADDRESS...
....
MOBILE # (Cell)..
HOME #..
WORK #..
FAX...
EMAIL...

NAME..
ADDRESS...
....
MOBILE # (Cell)..
HOME #..
WORK #..
FAX...
EMAIL...

NAME..
ADDRESS...
....
MOBILE # (Cell)..
HOME #..
WORK #..
FAX...
EMAIL...

NOTES:

NAME..
ADDRESS..
....
MOBILE # (Cell)...
HOME #..
WORK #...
FAX..
EMAIL..

NAME..
ADDRESS..
....
MOBILE # (Cell)...
HOME #..
WORK #...
FAX..
EMAIL..

NAME..
ADDRESS..
....
MOBILE # (Cell)...
HOME #..
WORK #...
FAX..
EMAIL..

NOTES:

NAME..
ADDRESS..
....
MOBILE # (Cell)...
HOME #..
WORK #..
FAX...
EMAIL...

NAME..
ADDRESS..
....
MOBILE # (Cell)...
HOME #..
WORK #..
FAX...
EMAIL...

NAME..
ADDRESS..
....
MOBILE # (Cell)...
HOME #..
WORK #..
FAX...
EMAIL...

NOTES: